WITH TRUMPET AND DRUM

With·Trumpet·and·Drum
by
Eugene·Field

Granger Index Reprint Series

 BOOKS FOR LIBRARIES PRESS
FREEPORT, NEW YORK

First Published 1892
Reprinted 1970

STANDARD BOOK NUMBER:

8369-6143-9

LIBRARY OF CONGRESS CATALOG CARD NUMBER:

70-116402

MANUFACTURED
BY
HALLMARK LITHOGRAPHERS, INC.
IN THE U.S.A.

This volume is made up of verse compiled from my "Little Book of Western Verse," my "Second Book of Verse," and the files of the "Chicago Daily News," the "Youth's Companion," and the "Ladies' Home Journal."

E. F.

CHICAGO, October 25, 1892.

WITH TRUMPET AND DRUM

With big tin trumpet and little red drum,
Marching like soldiers, the children come!
 It's this way and that way they circle and file —
  My! but that music of theirs is fine!
 This way and that way, and after a while
  They march straight into this heart of mine!
A sturdy old heart, but it has to succumb
To the blare of that trumpet and beat of that drum!

Come on, little people, from cot and from hall —
This heart it hath welcome and room for you all!
 It will sing you its songs and warm you with love,
  As your dear little arms with my arms intertwine;
 It will rock you away to the dreamland above —
  Oh, a jolly old heart is this old heart of mine,
And jollier still is it bound to become
When you blow that big trumpet and beat that red drum!

So come; though I see not his dear little face
And hear not his voice in this jubilant place,
 I know he were happy to bid me enshrine
  His memory deep in my heart with your play —
 Ah me! but a love that is sweeter than mine
  Holdeth my boy in its keeping to-day!
And my heart it is lonely — so, little folk, come,
March in and make merry with trumpet and drum!

                              EUGENE FIELD.

 Chicago, September 13, 1892.

* Cooing Dove.

CONTENTS

WITH TRUMPET AND DRUM

❦

THE SUGAR-PLUM TREE

Have you ever heard of the Sugar-Plum Tree?
  'T is a marvel of great renown!
It blooms on the shore of the Lollipop sea
  In the garden of Shut-Eye Town;
The fruit that it bears is so wondrously sweet
  (As those who have tasted it say)
That good little children have only to eat
  Of that fruit to be happy next day.

When you 've got to the tree, you would have
    a hard time
  To capture the fruit which I sing;
The tree is so tall that no person could climb
  To the boughs where the sugar-plums swing!

But up in that tree sits a chocolate cat,
  And a gingerbread dog prowls below —
And this is the way you contrive to get at
  Those sugar-plums tempting you so:

You say but the word to that gingerbread dog
  And he barks with such terrible zest
That the chocolate cat is at once all agog,
  As her swelling proportions attest.
And the chocolate cat goes cavorting around
  From this leafy limb unto that,
And the sugar-plums tumble, of course, to the
      ground —
    Hurrah for that chocolate cat!

There are marshmallows, gumdrops, and pep-
      permint canes,
  With stripings of scarlet or gold,
And you carry away of the treasure that rains
  As much as your apron can hold!

So come, little child, cuddle closer to me
  In your dainty white nightcap and gown,
And I 'll rock you away to that Sugar-Plum
    Tree
  In the garden of Shut-Eye Town.

KRINKEN

KRINKEN was a little child,—
    It was summer when he smiled.
Oft the hoary sea and grim
Stretched its white arms out to him,
Calling, "Sun-child, come to me;
Let me warm my heart with thee!"
But the child heard not the sea.

Krinken on the beach one day
Saw a maiden Nis at play;
Fair, and very fair, was she,
Just a little child was he.
"Krinken," said the maiden Nis,
"Let me have a little kiss,—
Just a kiss, and go with me
To the summer-lands that be
Down within the silver sea."

Krinken was a little child,
By the maiden Nis beguiled;
Down into the calling sea
With the maiden Nis went he.

But the sea calls out no more;
It is winter on the shore,—
Winter where that little child
Made sweet summer when he smiled:
Though 't is summer on the sea
Where with maiden Nis went he,—
Summer, summer evermore,—
It is winter on the shore,
Winter, winter evermore.

Of the summer on the deep
Come sweet visions in my sleep;
His fair face lifts from the sea,
His dear voice calls out to me,—
These my dreams of summer be.

Krinken was a little child,
By the maiden Nis beguiled;

Oft the hoary sea and grim
Reached its longing arms to him,
Crying, "Sun-child, come to me;
Let me warm my heart with thee!"
But the sea calls out no more;
It is winter on the shore,—
Winter, cold and dark and wild;
Krinken was a little child,—
It was summer when he smiled;
Down he went into the sea,
And the winter bides with me.
Just a little child was he.

THE NAUGHTY DOLL

MY dolly is a dreadful care,—
　Her name is Miss Amandy;
I dress her up and curl her hair,
　And feed her taffy candy.
Yet heedless of the pleading voice
　Of her devoted mother,
She will not wed her mother's choice,
　But says she 'll wed another.

I 'd have her wed the china vase,—
　There is no Dresden rarer;
You might go searching every place
　And never find a fairer.
He is a gentle, pinkish youth,—
　Of that there 's no denying;
Yet when I speak of him, forsooth,
　Amandy falls to crying!

She loves the drum—that 's very plain—
  And scorns the vase so clever;
And weeping, vows she will remain
  A spinster doll forever!
The protestations of the drum
  I am convinced are hollow;
When once distressing times should come,
  How soon would ruin follow!

Yet all in vain the Dresden boy
  From yonder mantel woos her;
A mania for that vulgar toy,
  The noisy drum, imbues her!
In vain I wheel her to and fro,
  And reason with her mildly,—
Her waxen tears in torrents flow,
  Her sawdust heart beats wildly.

I 'm sure that when I 'm big and tall,
  And wear long trailing dresses,
I sha'n't encourage beaux at all·
  Till mama acquiesces;

Our choice will be a suitor then
  As pretty as this vase is,—
Oh, how we 'll hate the noisy men
  With whiskers on their faces!

NIGHTFALL IN DORDRECHT

THE mill goes toiling slowly around
 With steady and solemn creak,
And my little one hears in the kindly sound
 The voice of the old mill speak.
While round and round those big white wings
 Grimly and ghostlike creep,
My little one hears that the old mill sings:
 "Sleep, little tulip, sleep!"

The sails are reefed and the nets are drawn,
 And, over his pot of beer,
The fisher, against the morrow's dawn,
 Lustily maketh cheer;
He mocks at the winds that caper along
 From the far-off clamorous deep—
But we—we love their lullaby song
 Of "Sleep, little tulip, sleep!"

Old dog Fritz in slumber sound
    Groans of the stony mart—
To-morrow how proudly he 'll trot you round,
    Hitched to our new milk-cart!
And you shall help me blanket the kine
    And fold the gentle sheep
And set the herring a-soak in brine—
    But now, little tulip, sleep!

A Dream-One comes to button the eyes
    That wearily droop and blink,
While the old mill buffets the frowning skies
    And scolds at the stars that wink;
Over your face the misty wings
    Of that beautiful Dream-One sweep,
And rocking your cradle she softly sings:
    "Sleep, little tulip, sleep!"

INTRY-MINTRY

WILLIE and Bess, Georgie and May—
Once, as these children were hard at play,
An old man, hoary and tottering, came
And watched them playing their pretty game.
He seemed to wonder, while standing there,
What the meaning thereof could be—
Aha, but the old man yearned to share
Of the little children's innocent glee
As they circled around with laugh and shout
And told their rime at counting out:
"Intry-mintry, cutrey-corn,
Apple-seed and apple-thorn;
Wire, brier, limber, lock,
Twelve geese in a flock;
Some flew east, some flew west,
Some flew over the cuckoo's nest!"

Willie and Bess, Georgie and May—
Ah, the mirth of that summer-day!
'T was Father Time who had come to share
The innocent joy of those children there;
  He learned betimes the game they played
    And into their sport with them went he—
  How *could* the children have been afraid,
    Since little they recked whom he might be?
They laughed to hear old Father Time
Mumbling that curious nonsense rime
    Of " Intry-mintry, cutrey-corn,
    Apple-seed and apple-thorn;
    Wire, brier, limber, lock,
    Twelve geese in a flock;
    Some flew east, some flew west,
    Some flew over the cuckoo's nest! "

Willie and Bess, Georgie and May,
And joy of summer — where are they?
The grim old man still standeth near
Crooning the song of a far-off year;

And into the winter I come alone,
    Cheered by that mournful requiem,
  Soothed by the dolorous monotone
      That shall count me off as it counted
        them —
The solemn voice of old Father Time
Chanting the homely nursery rime
      He learned of the children a summer morn
      When, with "apple-seed and apple-thorn,"
      Life was full of the dulcet cheer
      That bringeth the grace of heaven anear —
      The sound of the little ones hard at play —
      Willie and Bess, Georgie and May.

PITTYPAT AND TIPPYTOE

All day long they come and go —
  Pittypat and Tippytoe;
  Footprints up and down the hall,
    Playthings scattered on the floor,
  Finger-marks along the wall,
    Tell-tale smudges on the door —
By these presents you shall know
Pittypat and Tippytoe.

How they riot at their play!
And a dozen times a day
  In they troop, demanding bread —
    Only buttered bread will do,
  And that butter must be spread
    Inches thick with sugar too!
And I never can say "No,
Pittypat and Tippytoe!"

Sometimes there are griefs to soothe,
Sometimes ruffled brows to smooth;
  For (I much regret to say)
    Tippytoe and Pittypat
  Sometimes interrupt their play
    With an internecine spat;
Fie, for shame! to quarrel so —
Pittypat and Tippytoe!

Oh the thousand worrying things
Every day recurrent brings!
  Hands to scrub and hair to brush,
    Search for playthings gone amiss,
  Many a wee complaint to hush,
    Many a little bump to kiss;
Life seems one vain, fleeting show
To Pittypat and Tippytoe!

And when day is at an end,
There are little duds to mend:
  Little frocks are strangely torn,
    Little shoes great holes reveal,
  Little hose, but one day worn,
    Rudely yawn at toe and heel!

Who but *you* could work such woe,
Pittypat and Tippytoe?

But when comes this thought to me:
"Some there are that childless be,"
    Stealing to their little beds,
        With a love I cannot speak,
    Tenderly I stroke their heads —
        Fondly kiss each velvet cheek.
God help those who do not know
A Pittypat or Tippytoe!

On the floor and down the hall,
Rudely smutched upon the wall,
    There are proofs in every kind
        Of the havoc they have wrought,
    And upon my heart you 'd find
        Just such trade-marks, if you sought;
Oh, how glad I am 't is so,
Pittypat and Tippytoe!

BALOW, MY BONNIE

Hush, bonnie, dinna greit;
    Moder will rocke her sweete,—
    Balow, my boy!
When that his toile ben done,
Daddie will come anone,—·
Hush thee, my lyttel one;
    Balow, my boy!

Gin thou dost sleepe, perchaunce·
Fayries will come to daunce,—
    Balow, my boy!
Oft hath thy moder seene
Moonlight and mirkland queene
Daunce on thy slumbering een,—
    Balow, my boy!

Then droned a bomblebee
Saftly this songe to thee:
   "Balow, my boy!"

And a wee heather bell,
Pluckt from a fayry dell,
Chimed thee this rune hersell:
   "Balow, my boy!"

Soe, bonnie, dinna greit;
Moder doth rock her sweete,—
   Balow, my boy!
Give mee thy lyttel hand,
Moder will hold it and
Lead thee to balow land,—
   Balow, my boy!

THE HAWTHORNE CHILDREN

THE Hawthorne children — seven in all —
    Are famous friends of mine,
And with what pleasure I recall
How, years ago, one gloomy fall,
    I took a tedious railway line
And journeyed by slow stages down
Unto that sleepy seaport town
    (Albeit one worth seeing),
  Where Hildegarde, John, Henry, Fred,
And Beatrix and Gwendolen
And she that was the baby then —
    These famous seven, as aforesaid,
      Lived, moved, and had their being.

The Hawthorne children gave me such
    A welcome by the sea,
That the eight of us were soon in touch,
And though their mother marveled much,
    Happy as larks were we!

Egad I was a boy again
With Henry, John, and Gwendolen!
   And, oh! the funny capers
  I cut with Hildegarde and Fred!
The pranks we heedless children played,
The deafening, awful noise we made—
  'T would shock my family, if they read
   About it in the papers!

The Hawthorne children all were smart;
   The girls, as I recall,
Had comprehended every art
Appealing to the head and heart,
   The boys were gifted, all;
'T was Hildegarde who showed me how
To hitch the horse and milk a cow
   And cook the best of suppers;
  With Beatrix upon the sands
I sprinted daily, and was beat,
While Henry stumped me to the feat
  Of walking round upon my hands
   Instead of on my "uppers."

The Hawthorne children liked me best
    Of evenings, after tea;
For then, by general request,
I spun them yarns about the west—
    And *all* involving Me!
I represented how I 'd slain
The bison on the gore-smeared plain,
    And divers tales of wonder
   I told of how I 'd fought and bled .
In Injun scrimmages galore,
Till Mrs. Hawthorne quoth " No more ! "
   And packed her darlings off to bed
    To dream of blood and thunder !

They must have changed a deal since then :
    The misses tall and fair
And those three lusty, handsome men,
Would they be girls and boys again
    Were I to happen there,
Down in that spot beside the sea
Where we made such tumultuous glee

In dull autumnal weather?
Ah me! the years go swiftly by,
And yet how fondly I recall
The week when we were children all —
    Dear Hawthorne children, you and I —
        Just eight of us, together!

LITTLE BLUE PIGEON

SLEEP, little pigeon, and fold your wings—
 Little blue pigeon with velvet eyes;
Sleep to tne singing of mother-bird swinging—
 Swinging the nest where her little one lies.

Away out yonder I see a star—
 Silvery star with a tinkling song;
To the soft dew falling I hear it calling—
 Calling and tinkling the night along.

In through the window a moonbeam comes—
 Little gold moonbeam with misty wings;
All silently creeping, it asks: "Is he sleeping—
 Sleeping and dreaming while mother sings?"

Up from the sea there floats the sob
  Of the waves that are breaking upon the
      shore,
As though they were groaning in anguish, and
      moaning —
  Bemoaning the ship that shall come no more.

But sleep, little pigeon, and fold your wings —
  Little blue pigeon with mournful eyes;
Am I not singing? — see, I am swinging —
  Swinging the nest where my darling lies.

THE LYTTEL BOY

Some time there ben a lyttel boy
    That wolde not renne and play,
And helpless like that little tyke
    Ben allwais in the way.
"Goe, make you merrie with the rest,"
    His weary moder cried;
But with a frown he catcht her gown
    And hong untill her side.

That boy did love his moder well,
    Which spake him faire, I ween;
He loved to stand and hold her hand
    And ken her with his een;
His cosset bleated in the croft,
    His toys unheeded lay,—
He wolde not goe, but, tarrying soe,
    Ben allwais in the way.

Godde loveth children and doth gird
　　His throne with soche as these,
And he doth smile in plaisaunce while
　　They cluster at his knees;
And some time, when he looked on earth
　　And watched the bairns at play,
He kenned with joy a lyttel boy
　　Ben allwais in the way.

And then a moder felt her heart
　　How that it ben to-torne,
She kissed eche day till she ben gray
　　The shoon he use to worn;
No bairn let hold untill her gown
　　Nor played upon the floore,—
Godde's was the joy; a lyttel boy
　　Ben in the way no more!

TEENY-WEENY

EVERY evening, after tea,
  Teeny-Weeny comes to me,
And, astride my willing knee,
   Plies his lash and rides away;
Though that palfrey, all too spare,
Finds his burden hard to bear,
Teeny-Weeny does n't care;
   He commands, and I obey!

First it 's trot, and gallop then;
Now it 's back to trot again;
Teeny-Weeny likes it when
   He is riding fierce and fast.
Then his dark eyes brighter grow
And his cheeks are all aglow:
"More!" he cries, and never "Whoa!"
   Till the horse breaks down at last.

Oh, the strange and lovely sights
Teeny-Weeny sees of nights,
As he makes those famous flights
    On that wondrous horse of his!
Oftentimes before he knows,
Wearylike his eyelids close,
And, still smiling, off he goes
    Where the land of By-low is.

There he sees the folk of fay
Hard at ring-a-rosie play,
And he hears those fairies say:
    " Come, let 's chase him to and fro!"
But, with a defiant shout,
Teeny puts that host to rout;
Of this tale I make no doubt,
    Every night he tells it so.

So I feel a tender pride
In my boy who dares to ride
That fierce horse of his astride,
    Off into those misty lands;

And as on my breast he lies,
Dreaming in that wondrous wise,
I caress his folded eyes,
　Pat his little dimpled hands.

On a time he went away,
Just a little while to stay,
And I 'm not ashamed to say
　I was very lonely then;
Life without him was so sad,
You can fancy I was glad
And made merry when I had
　Teeny-Weeny. back again!

So of evenings, after tea,
When he toddles up to me
And goes tugging at my knee,
　You should hear his palfrey neigh!
You should see him prance and shy,
When, with an exulting cry,
Teeny-Weeny, vaulting high,
　Plies his lash and rides away!

NELLIE

His listening soul hears no echo of battle,
   No pæan of triumph nor welcome of fame;
But down through the years comes a little
      one's prattle,
   And softly he murmurs her idolized name.
And it seems as if now at his heart she were
      clinging
   As she clung in those dear, distant years to
         his knee;
He sees her fair face, and he hears her sweet
      singing —
   And Nellie is coming from over the sea.

While each patriot's hope stays the fullness of
      sorrow,
   While our eyes are bedimmed and our
         voices are low,

He dreams of the daughter who comes with
    the morrow
  Like an angel come back from the dear
    long ago.
Ah, what to him now is a nation's emotion,
  And what for our love or our grief careth he?
A swift-speeding ship is a-sail on the ocean,
  And Nellie is coming from over the sea!

O daughter — my daughter! when Death
    stands before me
  And beckons me off to that far misty shore,
Let me see your loved form bending tenderly
    o'er me,
  And feel your dear kiss on my lips as of yore.
In the grace of your love all my anguish abating,
  I 'll bear myself bravely and proudly as he,
And know the sweet peace that hallowed his
    waiting
  When Nellie was coming from over the sea.

NORSE LULLABY

THE sky is dark and the hills are white
As the storm-king speeds from the north
    to-night;
And this is the song the storm-king sings,
As over the world his cloak he flings:
    "Sleep, sleep, little one, sleep";
He rustles his wings and gruffly sings:
    "Sleep, little one, sleep."

On yonder mountain-side a vine
Clings at the foot of a mother pine;
The tree bends over the trembling thing,
And only the vine can hear her sing:
    "Sleep, sleep, little one, sleep—
What shall you fear when I am here?
    Sleep, little one, sleep."

The king may sing in his bitter flight,
The tree may croon to the vine to-night,
But the little snowflake at my breast
Liketh the song *I* sing the best—
    Sleep, sleep, little one, sleep;
Weary thou art, a-next my heart
    Sleep, little one, sleep.

GRANDMA'S PRAYER

I PRAY that, risen from the dead,
  I may in glory stand—
A crown, perhaps, upon my head,
  But a needle in my hand.

I 've never learned to sing or play,
  So let no harp be mine;
From birth unto my dying day,
  Plain sewing 's been my line.

Therefore, accustomed to the end
  To plying useful stitches,
I 'll be content if asked to mend
  The little angels' breeches.

SOME TIME

Last night, my darling, as you slept,
    I thought I heard you sigh,
And to your little crib I crept,
    And watched a space thereby;
Then, bending down, I kissed your brow —
    For, oh! I love you so —
You are too young to know it now,
    But some time you shall know.

Some time, when, in a darkened place
    Where others come to weep,
Your eyes shall see a weary face
    Calm in eternal sleep;
The speechless lips, the wrinkled brow,
    The patient smile may show —
You are too young to know it now,
    But some time you shall know.

Look backward, then, into the years,
　And see me here to-night—
See, O my darling! how my tears
　Are falling as I write;
And feel once more upon your brow
　The kiss of long ago—
You are too young to know it now,
　But some time you shall know.

THE FIRE-HANGBIRD'S NEST

As I am sitting in the sun upon the porch
    to-day,
I look with wonder at the elm that stands
    across the way;
I say and mean "with wonder," for now it
    seems to me
That elm is not as tall as years ago it used
    to be!
The old fire-hangbird 's built her nest therein
    for many springs —
High up amid the sportive winds the curious
    cradle swings,
But not so high as when a little boy I did
    my best
To scale that elm and carry off the old fire-
    hangbird's nest!

The Hubbard boys had tried in vain to reach
    the homely prize
That dangled from that upper outer twig in
    taunting wise,
And once, when Deacon Turner's boy had
    almost grasped the limb,
He fell! and had to have a doctor operate
    on him!
Philetus Baker broke his leg and Orrin Root
    his arm—
But what of that? The danger gave the
    sport a special charm!
The Bixby and the Cutler boys, the New-
    tons and the rest
Ran every risk to carry off the old fire-hang-
    bird's nest!

I can remember that I used to knee my
    trousers through,
That mother used to wonder how my legs
    got black and blue,

And how she used to talk to me and make
    stern threats when she
Discovered that my hobby was the nest in
    yonder tree;
How, as she patched my trousers or greased
    my purple legs,
She told me 't would be wicked to destroy a
    hangbird's eggs,
And then she 'd call on father and on gran'pa
    to attest
That they, as boys, had never robbed an old
    fire-hangbird's nest!

Yet all those years I coveted the trophy flaunt-
    ing there,
While, as it were in mockery of my abject
    despair,
The old fire-hangbird confidently used to
    come and go,
As if she were indifferent to the bandit horde
    below!

And sometimes clinging to her nest we thought
    we heard her chide
The callow brood whose cries betrayed the
    fear that reigned inside:
" Hush, little dears! all profitless shall be their
    wicked quest—
I knew my business when I built the old fire-
    hangbird's nest!"

For many, very many years that mother-bird
    has come
To rear her pretty little brood within that cozy
    home.
She is the selfsame bird of old—I 'm certain
    it is she—
Although the chances are that she has quite
    forgotten me.
Just as of old that prudent, crafty bird of com-
    pound name
(And in parenthesis I 'll say her nest is still
    the same);

Just as of old the passion, too, that fires the
    youthful breast
To climb unto and comprehend the old fire-
    hangbird's nest !

I like to see my old-time friend swing in that
    ancient tree,
And, if the elm 's as tall and sturdy as it *used*
    to be,
I 'm sure that many a year that nest shall in
    the breezes blow,
For boys are n't what they used to be a forty
    years ago !
The elm looks shorter than it did when bro-
    ther Rufe and I
Beheld with envious hearts that trophy flaunted
    from on high ;
He writes that in the city where he 's living
    'way out West
His little boys have never seen an old fire-
    hangbird's nest !

Poor little chaps! how lonesomelike their city
    life must be —
I wish they 'd come and live awhile in this
    old house with me!
They 'd have the honest friends and healthful
    sports I used to know
When brother Rufe and I were boys a forty
    years ago.
So, when they grew from romping lads to
    busy, useful men,
They could recall with proper pride their
    country life again;
And of those recollections of their youth I 'm
    sure the best
Would be of how they sought in vain the old
    fire-hangbird's nest!

BUTTERCUP, POPPY, FORGET-ME-NOT

BUTTERCUP, Poppy, Forget-me-not—
These three bloomed in a garden spot;
And once, all merry with song and play,
A little one heard three voices say:
"Shine and shadow, summer and spring,
    O thou child with the tangled hair
    And laughing eyes! we three shall bring
        Each an offering passing fair."
The little one did not understand,
But they bent and kissed the dimpled hand.

Buttercup gamboled all day long,
Sharing the little one's mirth and song;
Then, stealing along on misty gleams,
Poppy came bearing the sweetest dreams.

Playing and dreaming — and that was all
  Till once a sleeper would not awake;
Kissing the little face under the pall,
    We thought of the words the third flower
        spake;
And we found betimes in a hallowed spot
The solace and peace of Forget-me-not.

Buttercup shareth the joy of day,
Glinting with gold the hours of play;
Bringeth the poppy sweet repose,
When the hands would fold and the eyes
        would close;
  And after it all — the play and the sleep
    Of a little life — what cometh then?
  To the hearts that ache and the eyes that
        weep
    A new flower bringeth God's peace again.
Each one serveth its tender lot —
Buttercup, Poppy, Forget-me-not.

WYNKEN, BLYNKEN, AND NOD

WYNKEN, Blynken, and Nod one night
   Sailed off in a wooden shoe —
Sailed on a river of crystal light,
   Into a sea of dew.
"Where are you going, and what do you
      wish?"
   The old moon asked the three.
"We have come to fish for the herring fish
   That live in this beautiful sea;
   Nets of silver and gold have we!"
         Said Wynken,
         Blynken,
         And Nod.

The old moon laughed and sang a song,
   As they rocked in the wooden shoe,
And the wind that sped them all night long
   Ruffled the waves of dew.

The little stars were the herring fish
    That lived in that beautiful sea —
"Now cast your nets wherever you wish —
    Never afeard are we ";
    So cried the stars to the fishermen three :
           Wynken,
           Blynken,
           And Nod.

All night long their nets they threw
    To the stars in the twinkling foam —
Then down from the skies came the wooden shoe,
    Bringing the fishermen home ;
'T was all so pretty a sail it seemed
    As if it could not be,
And some folks thought 't was a dream they'd
        dreamed
    Of sailing that beautiful sea —
    But I shall name you the fishermen three :
           Wynken,
           Blynken,
           And Nod.

Wynken and Blynken are two little eyes,
    And Nod is a little head,
And the wooden shoe that sailed the skies
    Is a wee one's trundle-bed.
So shut your eyes while mother sings
    Of wonderful sights that be,
And you shall see the beautiful things
    As you rock in the misty sea,
    Where the old shoe rocked the fishermen
        three :
            Wynken,
            Blynken,
            And Nod.

GOLD AND LOVE FOR DEARIE

OUT on the mountain over the town,
  All night long, all night long,
The trolls go up and the trolls go down,
  Bearing their packs and singing a song;
And this is the song the hill-folk croon,
As they trudge in the light of the misty
      moon—
This is ever their dolorous tune:
" Gold, gold! ever more gold—
      Bright red gold for dearie!"

Deep in the hill a father delves
  All night long, all night long;
None but the peering, furtive elves
  Sees his toil and hears his song;

Merrily ever the cavern rings
As merrily ever his pick he swings,
And merrily ever this song he sings:
" Gold, gold! ever more gold—
      Bright red gold for dearie!"

Mother is rocking thy lowly bed
    All night long, all night long,
Happy to smooth thy curly head,
    To hold thy hand and to sing *her* song:
'T is not of the hill-folk dwarfed and old,
Nor the song of thy father, stanch and bold,
And the burthen it beareth is not of gold:
But it 's " Love, love! nothing but love—
    Mother's love for dearie!"

THE PEACE OF CHRISTMAS-TIME

Dearest, how hard it is to say
That all is for the best,
Since, sometimes, in a grievous way
God's will is manifest.

See with what hearty, noisy glee
Our little ones to-night
Dance round and round our Christmas tree
With pretty toys bedight.

Dearest, one voice they may not hear,
One face they may not see—
Ah, what of all this Christmas cheer
Cometh to you and me?

Cometh before our misty eyes
    That other little face,
And we clasp, in tender, reverent wise,
    That love in the old embrace.

Dearest, the Christ-Child walks to-night,
    Bringing his peace to men,
And he bringeth to you and to me the light
    Of the old, old years again.

Bringeth the peace of long ago,
    When a wee one clasped your knee
And lisped of the morrow — dear one, **you**
        know —
    And here come back is he !

Dearest, 't is sometimes hard to say
    That all is for the best,
For, often, in a grievous way
    God's will is manifest.

But in the grace of this holy night
  That bringeth us back our child,
Let us see that the ways of God are right,
  And so be reconciled.

TO A LITTLE BROOK

YOU 'RE not so big as you were then,
  O little brook! —
I mean those hazy summers when
We boys roamed, full of awe, beside
Your noisy, foaming, tumbling tide,
And wondered if it could be true
That there were bigger brooks than you,
  O mighty brook, O peerless brook!

All up and down this reedy place
  Where lives the brook,
We angled for the furtive dace;
The redwing-blackbird did his best
To make us think he 'd built his nest
Hard by the stream, when, like as not,
He 'd hung it in a secret spot
  Far from the brook, the telltale brook!

And often, when the noontime heat
　　Parboiled the brook,
We 'd draw our boots and swing our feet
Upon the waves that, in their play,
Would tag us last and scoot away;
And mother never seemed to know
What burnt our legs and chapped them so—
　　But father guessed it was the brook!

And Fido—how he loved to swim
　　The cooling brook,
Whenever we 'd throw sticks for him;
And how we boys *did* wish that we
Could only swim as good as he—
Why, Daniel Webster never was
Recipient of such great applause
　　As Fido, battling with the brook!

But once—O most unhappy day
　　For you, my brook!—
Came Cousin Sam along that way;

And, having lived a spell out West,
Where creeks are n't counted much at best,
He neither waded, swam, nor leapt,
But, with superb indifference, *stept*
    Across that brook — our mighty brook!

Why do you scamper on your way,
    You little brook,
When I come back to you to-day?
Is it because you flee the grass
That lunges at you as you pass,
As if, in playful mood, it would
Tickle the truant if it could,
    You chuckling brook — you saucy brook?

Or is it you no longer know —
    You fickle brook —
The honest friend of long ago?
The years that kept us twain apart
Have changed my face, but not my heart —
Many and sore those years, and yet
I fancied you could not forget
    That happy time, my playmate brook!

Oh, sing again in artless glee,
  My little brook,
The song you used to sing for me —
The song that 's lingered in my ears
So soothingly these many years;
My grief shall be forgotten when
I hear your tranquil voice again
  And that sweet song, dear little brook!

CROODLIN' DOO

Ho, pretty bee, did you see my croodlin' doo?
 Ho, little lamb, is she jinkin' on the lea?
  Ho, bonnie fairy, bring my dearie back
   to me —
Got a lump o' sugar an' a posie for you,
Only bring me back my wee, wee croodlin' doo!

Why! here you are, my little croodlin' doo!
 Looked in er cradle, but did n't find you
  there —
 Looked f'r my wee, wee croodlin' doo
  ever'where;
Be'n kind lonesome all er day withouten you —
Where you be'n, my teeny, wee, wee croodlin'
 doo?

Now you go balow, my little croodlin' doo;
　　Now you go rockaby ever so far,—
　　Rockaby, rockaby up to the star
That 's winkin' an' blinkin' an' singin' to you,
As you go balow, my wee, wee croodlin' doo!

LITTLE MISTRESS SANS-MERCI

LITTLE Mistress Sans-Merci
    Fareth world-wide, fancy free:
Trotteth cooing to and fro,
    And her cooing is command—
Never ruled there yet, I trow,
    Mightier despot in the land.
And my heart it lieth where
Mistress Sans-Merci doth fare.

Little Mistress Sans-Merci—
She hath made a slave of me!
"Go," she biddeth, and I go—
    "Come," and I am fain to come—
Never mercy doth she show,
    Be she wroth or frolicsome,
Yet am I content to be
Slave to Mistress Sans-Merci!

Little Mistress Sans-Merci
Hath become so dear to me
  That I count as passing sweet
    All the pain her moods impart,
  And I bless the little feet
    That go trampling on my heart:
Ah, how lonely life would be
But for little Sans-Merci!

Little Mistress Sans-Merci,
Cuddle close this night to me,
  And the heart, which all day long
    Ruthless thou hast trod upon,
  Shall outpour a soothing song
    For its best belovéd one—
All its tenderness for thee,
Little Mistress Sans-Merci!

LONG AGO

I ONCE knew all the birds that came
  And nested in our orchard trees,
For every flower I had a name—
  My friends were woodchucks, toads, and bees;
I knew where thrived in yonder glen
  What plants would soothe a stone-bruised
      toe—
Oh, I was very learned then,
  But that was very long ago.

I knew the spot upon the hill
  Where checkerberries could be found,
I knew the rushes near the mill
  Where pickerel lay that weighed a pound!

I knew the wood — the very tree
  Where lived the poaching, saucy crow,
And all the woods and crows knew me —
  But that was very long ago.

And pining for the joys of youth,
  I tread the old familiar spot
Only to learn this solemn truth:
  I have forgotten, am forgot.
Yet here 's this youngster at my knee
  Knows all the things I used to know;
To think I once was wise as he! —
  But that was very long ago.

I know it 's folly to complain
  Of whatsoe'er the fates decree,
Yet, were not wishes all in vain,
  I tell you what my wish should be:
I 'd wish to be a boy again,
  Back with the friends I used to know.
For I was, oh, so happy then —
  But that was very long ago!

IN THE FIRELIGHT

THE fire upon the hearth is low,
 And there is stillness everywhere,
  And, like wing'd spirits, here and there
The firelight shadows fluttering go.
And as the shadows round me creep,
 A childish treble breaks the gloom,
  And softly from a further room
Comes: "Now I lay me down to sleep."

And, somehow, with that little pray'r
 And that sweet treble in my ears,
  My thought goes back to distant years,
And lingers with a dear one there;

And as I hear my child's amen,
  My mother's faith comes back to me—
  Crouched at her side I seem to be,
And mother holds my hands again.

Oh, for an hour in that dear place—
  Oh, for the peace of that dear time—
  Oh, for that childish trust sublime—
Oh, for a glimpse of mother's face!
Yet, as the shadows round me creep,
  I do not seem to be alone—
  Sweet magic of that treble tone
And " Now I lay me down to sleep ! "

COBBLER AND STORK

Cobbler.

STORK, I am justly wroth,
  For thou hast wronged me sore;
The ash roof-tree that shelters thee
  Shall shelter thee no more!

Stork.

Full fifty years I 've dwelt
  Upon this honest tree,
And long ago (as people know!)
  I brought thy father thee.
What hail hath chilled thy heart,
  That thou shouldst bid me go?
Speak out, I pray — then I 'll away,
  Since thou commandest so.

Cobbler.

Thou tellest of the time
 When, wheeling from the west,
This hut thou sought'st and one
  thou brought'st
 Unto a mother's breast.
I was the wretched child
 Was fetched that dismal morn—
'T were better die than be (as I)
 To life of misery born!
And hadst thou borne me on
 Still farther up the town,
A king I 'd be of high degree,
 And wear a golden crown!
For yonder lives the prince
 Was brought that selfsame day:
How happy he, while—look at me!
 I toil my life away!
And see my little boy—
 To what estate he 's born!
Why, when I die no hoard leave I
 But poverty and scorn.
And *thou* hast done it all—

I might have been a king
And ruled in state, but for thy hate,
   Thou base, perfidious thing !

Stork.

Since, cobbler, thou dost speak
   Of one thou lovest well,
Hear of that king what grievous thing
   This very morn befell.
Whilst round thy homely bench
   They well-belovéd played,
In yonder hall beneath a pall
   A little one was laid;
Thy well-belovéd's face
   Was rosy with delight,
But 'neath that pall in yonder hall
   The little face is white;
Whilst by a merry voice
   Thy soul is filled with cheer,
Another weeps for one that sleeps
   All mute and cold anear;
One father hath his hope,

And one is childless now;
He wears a crown and rules a town—
Only a cobbler *thou !*
Wouldst thou exchange thy lot
At price of such a woe ?
I 'll nest no more above thy door,
But, as thou bidst me, go.

Cobbler.

Nay, stork ! thou shalt remain—
I mean not what I said;
Good neighbors we must always be,
So make thy home o'erhead.
I would not change my bench
For any monarch's throne,
Nor sacrifice at any price
My darling and my own !
Stork ! on my roof-tree bide,
That, seeing thee anear,
I 'll thankful be God sent by thee
Me and my darling here !

"LOLLYBY, LOLLY, LOLLYBY"

Last night, whiles that the curfew bell ben
      ringing,
I heard a moder to her dearie singing
    " Lollyby, lolly, lollyby ";
And presently that chylde did cease hys weeping,
And on his moder's breast did fall a-sleeping
    To "lolly, lolly, lollyby."

Faire ben the chylde unto his moder clinging,
But fairer yet the moder's gentle singing—
    " Lollyby, lolly, lollyby ";
And angels came and kisst the dearie smiling
In dreems while him hys moder ben beguiling
    With "lolly, lolly, lollyby."

70

Then to my harte saies I : " Oh, that thy
    beating
Colde be assuaged by some sweete voice re-
    peating
    ' Lollyby, lolly, lollyby ';
That like this lyttel chylde I, too, ben sleeping
With plaisaunt phantasies about me creeping,
    To ' lolly, lolly, lollyby '! "

Some time,— mayhap when curfew bells are
    ringing —
A weary harte shall heare straunge voices
    singing
    " Lollyby, lolly, lollyby ";
Some time, mayhap, with Chryst's love round
    me streaming,
I shall be lulled into eternal dreeming,
    With " lolly, lolly, lollyby."

LIZZIE AND THE BABY

I WONDER ef all wimmin air
 Like Lizzie is when we go out
To theaters an' concerts where
 Is things the papers talk about.
Do other wimmin fret an' stew
 Like they wuz bein' crucified —
Frettin' a show or concert through,
 With wonderin' ef the baby cried?

Now Lizzie knows that gran'ma 's there
 To see that everything is right,
Yet Lizzie thinks that gran'ma's care
 Ain't good enuff f'r baby, quite;
Yet what am I to answer when
 She kind uv fidgets at my side,
An' asks me every now and then :
 " I wonder if the baby cried ? "

Seems like she seen two little eyes
　　A-pinin' f'r their mother's smile—
Seems like she heern the pleadin' cries
　　Uv one she thinks uv all the while;
An' so she 's sorry that she come,
　　An' though she allus tries to hide
The truth, she 'd ruther stay to hum
　　Than wonder ef the baby cried.

Yes, wimmin folks is all alike—
　　By Lizzie you kin jedge the rest;
There never wuz a little tyke,
　　But that his mother loved him best.
And nex' to bein' what I be—
　　The husband uv my gentle bride—
I 'd wisht I wuz that croodlin' wee,
　　With Lizzie wonderin' ef I cried.

AT THE DOOR

I THOUGHT myself, indeed, secure
  So fast the door, so firm the lock;
But, lo! he toddling comes to lure
  My parent ear with timorous knock.

My heart were stone could it withstand
  The sweetness of my baby's plea,—
That timorous, baby knocking and
  "Please let me in,—it 's only me."

I threw aside the unfinished book,
  Regardless of its tempting charms,
And, opening wide the door, I took
  My laughing darling in my arms.

Who knows but in Eternity,
   I, like a truant child, shall wait
The glories of a life to be,
   Beyond the Heavenly Father's gate?

And will that Heavenly Father heed
   The truant's supplicating cry,
As at the outer door I plead,
   " 'T is I, O Father! only I?"

HUGO'S "CHILD AT PLAY"

A CHILD was singing at his play—
　　I heard the song, and paused to hear;
His mother moaning, groaning lay,
　　And, lo! a specter stood anear!

The child shook sunlight from his hair,
　　And caroled gaily all day long—
Aye, with that specter gloating there,
　　The innocent made mirth and song!

How like to harvest fruit wert thou,
　　O sorrow, in that dismal room—
God ladeth not the tender bough
　　Save with the joy of bud and bloom!

HI-SPY

STRANGE that the city thoroughfare,
  Noisy and bustling all the day,
Should with the night renounce its care
  And lend itself to children's play!

Oh, girls are girls, and boys are boys,
  And have been so since Abel's birth,
And shall be so till dolls and toys
  Are with the children swept from earth.

The selfsame sport that crowns the day
  Of many a Syrian shepherd's son,
Beguiles the little lads at play
  By night in stately Babylon.

I hear their voices in the street,
  Yet 't is so different now from then!
Come, brother! from your winding-sheet,
  And let us two be boys again!

LITTLE BOY BLUE

THE little toy dog is covered with dust,
　But sturdy and stanch he stands;
And the little toy soldier is red with rust,
　And his musket molds in his hands.
Time was when the little toy dog was new,
　And the soldier was passing fair;
And that was the time when our Little Boy Blue
　Kissed them and put them there.

"Now, don't you go till I come," he said,
　"And don't you make any noise!"
So, toddling off to his trundle-bed,
　He dreamt of the pretty toys;
And, as he was dreaming, an angel song
　Awakened our Little Boy Blue —
Oh! the years are many, the years are long,
　But the little toy friends are true!

Aye, faithful to Little Boy Blue they stand,
   Each in the same old place —
Awaiting the touch of a little hand,
   The smile of a little face;
And they wonder, as waiting the long years
      through
   In the dust of that little chair,
What has become of our Little Boy Blue,
   Since he kissed them and put them there.

FATHER'S LETTER

I 'M going to write a letter to our oldest boy
who went
Out West last spring to practise law and run
for president;
I 'll tell him all the gossip I guess he 'd like
to hear,
For he has n't seen the home-folks for going
on a year!
Most generally it 's Marthy does the writing,
but as she
Is suffering with a felon, why, the job devolves
on me —
So, when the supper things are done and put
away to-night,
I 'll draw my boots and shed my coat and
settle down to write.

I 'll tell him crops are looking up, with pros-
    pects big for corn,
That, fooling with the barnyard gate, the off-
    ox hurt his horn;
That the Templar lodge is doing well — Tim
    Bennett joined last week
When the prohibition candidate for Congress
    came to speak;
That the old gray woodchuck 's living still
    down in the pasture-lot,
A-wondering what 's become of little William,
    like as not!
Oh, yes, there 's lots of pleasant things and
    no bad news to tell,
Except that old Bill Graves was sick, but now
    he 's up and well.

Cy Cooper says — (but I 'll not pass my word
    that it is so,
For Cy he is some punkins on spinning yarns,
    you know) —
He says that, since the freshet, the pickerel
    are so thick

In Baker's pond you can wade in and kill
  'em with a stick!
The Hubbard girls are teaching school, and
  Widow Cutler's Bill
Has taken Eli Baxter's place in Luther East-
  man's mill;
Old Deacon Skinner's dog licked Deacon
  Howard's dog last week,
And now there are two lambkins in one flock
  that will not speak.

The yellow rooster froze his feet, a-wadin'
  through the snow,
And now he leans agin the fence when he
  starts in to crow;
The chestnut colt that was so skittish when
  he went away—
I 've broke him to the sulky and I drive him
  every day!
We 've got pink window curtains for the front
  spare-room up-stairs,
And Lizzie 's made new covers for the parlor
  lounge and chairs;

We 've roofed the barn and braced the elm
    that has the hangbird's nest —
Oh, there 's been lots of changes since our
    William went out West!

Old Uncle Enos Packard is getting mighty
    gay —
He gave Miss Susan Birchard a peach the
    other day!
His late lamented Sarah hain't been buried
    quite a year,
So his purring 'round Miss Susan causes criti-
    cism here.
At the last donation party, the minister opined
That, if he 'd half suspicioned what was com-
    ing, he 'd resigned;
For, though they brought him slippers like he
    was a centipede,
His pantry was depleted by the consequential
    feed!
'These are the things I 'll write him — our boy
    that 's in the West;

And I 'll tell him how we miss him—his
    mother and the rest;
Why, we never have an apple-pie that mother
    does n't say:
" *He* liked it so—I wish that he could have
    a piece to-day!"
I 'll tell him we are prospering, and hope he
    is the same—
That we hope he 'll have no trouble getting
    on to wealth and fame;
And just before I write " good-by from father
    and the rest,"
I 'll say that "mother sends her love," and
    that will please him best.

For when *I* went away from home, the weekly
    news I heard
Was nothing to the tenderness I found in that
    one word—
The sacred name of mother—why, even now
    as then,
The thought brings back the saintly face, the
    gracious love again;

And in my bosom seems to come a peace that
    is divine,

As if an angel spirit communed a while with
    mine;

And one man's heart is strengthened by the
    message from above,

And earth seems nearer heaven when "mother
    sends her love."

JEWISH LULLABY

My harp is on the willow-tree,
　　Else would I sing, O love, to thee
　　　　A song of long-ago —
Perchance the song that Miriam sung
Ere yet Judea's heart was wrung
　　　　By centuries of woe.

I ate my crust in tears to-day,
As scourged I went upon my way —
　　　　And yet my darling smiled;
Aye, beating at my breast, he laughed —
My anguish curdled not the draught —
　　　　'T was sweet with love, my child!

The shadow of the centuries lies
Deep in thy dark and mournful eye
    But, hush! and close them now;
And in the dreams that thou shalt dream
The light of other days shall seem
    To glorify thy brow!

Our harp is on the willow-tree—
I have no song to sing to thee,
    As shadows round us roll;
But, hush and sleep, and thou shalt hear
Jehovah's voice that speaks to cheer
    Judea's fainting soul!

OUR WHIPPINGS

COME, Harvey, let us sit a while and talk
about the times
Before you went to selling clothes and I to
peddling rimes —
The days when we were little boys, as naughty
little boys
As ever worried home-folks with their ever-
lasting noise!
Egad! and, were we so disposed, I 'll venture
we could show
The scars of wallopings we got some forty
years ago;
What wallopings I mean I think I need not
specify —
Mother's whippings did n't hurt, but father's!
oh, my!

The way that we played hookey those many
    years ago —
We 'd rather give 'most anything than have
    our children know!
The thousand naughty things we did, the
    thousand fibs we told —
Why, thinking of them makes my presbyte-
    rian blood run cold!
How often Deacon Sabine Morse remarked
    if we were his
He 'd tan our " pesky little hides until the
    blisters riz!"
It 's many a hearty thrashing to that Deacon
    Morse we owe —
Mother's whippings did n't count — father's did,
    though!

We used to sneak off swimmin' in those care-
    less, boyish days,
And come back home of evenings with our
    necks and backs ablaze;
How mother used to wonder why our clothes
    were full of sand,

But father, having been a boy, appeared to
    understand.
And, after tea, he 'd beckon us to join him
    in the shed
Where he 'd proceed to tinge our backs a
    deeper, darker red;
Say what we will of mother's, there is none
    will controvert
The proposition that our father's lickings al-
    ways hurt!

For mother was by nature so forgiving and
    so mild
That she inclined to spare the rod although
    she spoiled the child;
And when at last in self-defense she had to
    whip us, she
Appeared to feel those whippings a great deal
    more than we!
But how we bellowed and took on, as if we 'd
    like to die —
Poor mother really thought she hurt, and that 's
    what made *her* cry!

Then how we youngsters snickered as out the
door we slid,
For mother's whippings never hurt, though
father's always did.

In after years poor father simmered down to
five feet four,
But in our youth he seemed to us in height
eight feet or more!
Oh, how we shivered when he quoth in cold,
suggestive tone:
"I 'll see you in the woodshed after supper all
alone!"
Oh, how the legs and arms and dust and trouser
buttons flew —
What florid vocalisms marked that vesper inter-
view!
Yes, after all this lapse of years, I feelingly assert,
With all respect to mother, it was father's whippings hurt!

The little boy experiencing that tingling 'neath
his vest
Is often loath to realize that all is for the best;

Yet, when the boy gets older, he pictures with
    delight
The buffetings of childhood—as we do here
    to-night.
The years, the gracious years, have smoothed
    and beautified the ways
That to our little feet seemed all too rugged
    in the days
Before you went to selling clothes and I to
    peddling rimes—
So, Harvey, let us sit a while and think upon
    those times.

THE ARMENIAN MOTHER

I WAS a mother, and I weep;
　　The night is come—the day is sped—
The night of woe profound, for, oh,
　　My little golden son is dead!

The pretty rose that bloomed anon
　　Upon my mother breast, they stole;
They let the dove I nursed with love
　　Fly far away—so sped my soul!

That falcon Death swooped down upon
　　My sweet-voiced turtle as he sung;
'T is hushed and dark where soared the lark,
　　And so, and so my heart was wrung!

93

Before my eyes, they sent the hail
  Upon my green pomegranate-tree —
Upon the bough where only now
  A rosy apple bent to me.

They shook my beauteous almond-tree,
  Beating its glorious bloom to death —
They strewed it round upon the ground,
  And mocked its fragrant dying breath.

I was a mother, and I weep;
  I seek the rose where nestleth none —
No more is heard the singing bird —
  I have no little golden son!

So fall the shadows over me,
  The blighted garden, lonely nest.
Reach down in love, O God above!
  And fold my darling to thy breast.

HEIGHO, MY DEARIE

A MOONBEAM floateth from the skies,
  Whispering: " Heigho, my dearie;
I would spin a web before your eyes—
A beautiful web of silver light
Wherein is many a wondrous sight
Of a radiant garden leagues away,
Where the softly tinkling lilies sway
And the snow-white lambkins are at play—
    Heigho, my dearie!"

A brownie stealeth from the vine,
    Singing: " Heigho, my dearie;
And will you hear this song of mine—
A song of the land of murk and mist
Where bideth the bud the dew hath kist?

Then let the moonbeam's web of light
Be spun before thee silvery white,
And I shall sing the livelong night —
    Heigho, my dearie!"

The night wind speedeth from the sea,
    Murmuring: "Heigho, my dearie;
I bring a mariner's prayer for thee;
So let the moonbeam veil thine eyes,
And the brownie sing thee lullabies —
But I shall rock thee to and fro,
Kissing the brow *he* loveth so.
And the prayer shall guard thy bed, I trow —
    Heigho, my dearie!"

TO A USURPER

Aha! a traitor in the camp,
   A rebel strangely bold,—
A lisping, laughing, toddling scamp,
   Not more than four years old!

To think that I, who 've ruled alone
   So proudly in the past,
Should be ejected from my throne
   By my own son at last!

He trots his treason to and fro,
   As only babies can,
And says he 'll be his mamma's beau
   When he 's a " gweat, big man"!

You stingy boy! you 've always had
   A share in mamma's heart.
Would you begrudge your poor old dad
   The tiniest little part?

That mamma, I regret to see,
　　Inclines to take your part,—
As if a dual monarchy
　　Should rule her gentle heart!

But when the years of youth have sped,
　　The bearded man, I trow,
Will quite forget he ever said
　　He 'd be his mamma's beau.

Renounce your treason, little son,
　　Leave mamma's heart to me;
For there will come another one
　　To claim your loyalty.

And when that other comes to you,
　　God grant her love may shine
Through all your life, as fair and true
　　As mamma's does through mine!

THE BELL-FLOWER TREE

WHEN brother Bill and I were boys,
  How often in the summer we
Would seek the shade your branches made,
  O fair and gracious bell-flower tree!
Amid the clover bloom we sat
  And looked upon the Holyoke range,
While Fido lay a space away,
  Thinking our silence very strange.

The woodchuck in the pasture-lot,
  Beside his furtive hole elate,
Heard, off beyond the pickerel pond,
  The redwing-blackbird chide her mate.
The bumblebee went bustling round,
  Pursuing labors never done —
With drone and sting, the greedy thing
  Begrudged the sweets we lay upon!

Our eyes looked always at the hills—
    The Holyoke hills that seemed to stand
Between us boys and pictured joys
    Of conquest in a further land!
Ah, how we coveted the time
    When we should leave this prosy place
And work our wills beyond those hills,
    And meet creation face to face!

You must have heard our childish talk—
    Perhaps our prattle gave you pain;
For then, old friend, you seemed to bend
    Your kindly arms about us twain.
It might have been the wind that sighed,
    And yet I thought I heard you say:
"Seek not the ills beyond those hills—
    Oh, stay with me, my children, stay!"

See, I 've come back; the boy you knew
    Is wiser, older, sadder grown;
I come once more, just as of yore—
    I come, but see! I come alone!

The memory of a brother's love,
  Of blighted hopes, I bring with me,
And here I lay my heart to-day —
  A weary heart, O bell-flower tree!

So let me nestle in your shade
  As though I were a boy again,
And pray extend your arms, old friend
  And love me as you used to then.
Sing softly as you used to sing,
  And maybe I shall seem to be
A little boy and feel the joy
  Of thy repose, O bell-flower tree!

FAIRY AND CHILD

OH, listen, little Dear-My-Soul,
  To the fairy voices calling,
For the moon is high in the misty sky
  And the honey dew is falling;
To the midnight feast in the clover bloom
  The bluebells are a-ringing,
And it 's " Come away to the land of fay "
  That the katydid is singing.

Oh, slumber, little Dear-My-Soul,
  And hand in hand we 'll wander—
Hand in hand to the beautiful land
  Of Balow, away off yonder;
Or we 'll sail along in a lily leaf
  Into the white moon's halo—
Over a stream of mist and dream
  Into the land of Balow.

Or, you shall have two beautiful wings—
  Two gossamer wings and airy,
And all the while shall the old moon smile
  And think you a little fairy;
And you shall dance in the velvet sky,
  And the silvery stars shall twinkle
And dream sweet dreams as over their beams
  Your footfalls softly tinkle.

THE GRANDSIRE

I LOVED him so; his voice had grown
Into my heart, and now to hear
The pretty song he had sung so long
Die on the lips to me so dear!
He a child with golden curls,
And I with head as white as snow —
I knelt down there and made this pray'r:
"God, let me be the first to go!"

How often I recall it now:
My darling tossing on his bed,
I sitting there in mute despair,
Smoothing the curls that crowned his head.
They did not speak to me of death —
A feeling *here* had told me so;
What could I say or do but pray
That I might be the first to go?

Yet, thinking of him standing there
  Out yonder as the years go by,
Waiting for me to come, I see
  'T was better he should wait, not I.
For when I walk the vale of death,
  Above the wail of Jordan's flow
Shall rise a song that shall make me strong—
  The call of the child that was first to go.

HUSHABY, SWEET MY OWN

FAIR is the castle up on the hill—
   Hushaby, sweet my own!
The night is fair, and the waves are still,
And the wind is singing to you and to me
In this lowly home beside the sea—
   Hushaby, sweet my own!

On yonder hill is store of wealth—
   Hushaby, sweet my own!
And revelers drink to a little one's health;
But you and I bide night and day
For the other love that has sailed away—
   Hushaby, sweet my own!

See not, dear eyes, the forms that creep
   Ghostlike, O my own!
Out of the mists of the murmuring deep;
Oh, see them not and make no cry
Till the angels of death have passed us by—
   Hushaby, sweet my own!

Ah, little they reck of you and me —
  Hushaby, sweet my own!
In our lonely home beside the sea;
They seek the castle up on the hill,
And there they will do their ghostly will —
  Hushaby, O my own!

Here by the sea a mother croons
  "Hushaby, sweet my own!"
In yonder castle a mother swoons
While the angels go down to the misty deep,
Bearing a little one fast asleep —
  Hushaby, sweet my own!

CHILD AND MOTHER

O MOTHER-MY-LOVE, if you 'll give me your
    hand,
  And go where I ask you to wander,
I will lead you away to a beautiful land—
  The Dreamland that 's waiting out yonder.
We 'll walk in a sweet-posie garden out there
  Where moonlight and starlight are streaming
And the flowers and the birds are filling the air
  With the fragrance and music of dreaming.

There 'll be no little tired-out boy to undress,
  No questions or cares to perplex you;
There 'll be no little bruises or bumps to caress,
  Nor patching of stockings to vex you.
For I 'll rock you away on a silver-dew stream,
  And sing you asleep when you 're weary,
And no one shall know of our beautiful dream
  But you and your own little dearie.

And when I am tired I 'll nestle my head
In the bosom that 's soothed me so often,
And the wide-awake stars shall sing in my
stead
A song which our dreaming shall soften.
So, Mother-My-Love, let me take your dear
hand,
And away through the starlight we 'll wan-
der —
Away through the mist to the beautiful land —
The Dreamland that 's waiting out yonder!

MEDIEVAL EVENTIDE SONG

COME hither, lyttel childe, and lie upon my
    breast to-night,
For yonder fares an angell yclad in raimaunt
    white,
And yonder sings ye angell as onely angells
    may,
And his songe ben of a garden that bloometh
    farre awaye.

To them that have no lyttel childe Godde
    sometimes sendeth down
A lyttel childe that ben a lyttel angell of his
    owne;
And if so bee they love that childe, he will-
    eth it to staye,
But elsewise, in his mercie, he taketh it awaye.

And sometimes, though they love it, Godde
    yearneth for ye childe,
And sendeth angells singing, whereby it ben
    beguiled;
They fold their arms about ye lamb that
    croodleth at his play,
And beare him to ye garden that bloometh
    farre awaye.

I wolde not lose ye lyttel lamb that Godde
    hath lent to me;
If I colde sing that angell songe, how joy-
    some I sholde be!
For, with mine arms about him, and my mu-
    sick in his eare,
What angell songe of paradize soever sholde I
    feare?

Soe come, my lyttel childe, and lie upon my
    breast to-night,
For yonder fares an angell yclad in raimaunt
    white,

And yonder sings that angell, as onely angells
    may,
And his songe ben of a garden that bloom-
    eth farre awaye.

ARMENIAN LULLABY

IF thou wilt shut thy drowsy eyes,
  My mulberry one, my golden sun!
The rose shall sing thee lullabies,
  My pretty cosset lambkin!
And thou shalt swing in an almond-tree,
With a flood of moonbeams rocking thee—
A silver boat in a golden sea,
  My velvet love, my nestling dove,
    My own pomegranate blossom!

The stork shall guard thee passing well
  All night, my sweet! my dimple-feet!
And bring thee myrrh and asphodel,
  My gentle rain-of-springtime!

And for thy slumbrous play shall twine
The diamond stars with an emerald vine
To trail in the waves of ruby wine,
  My myrtle bloom, my heart's perfume,
    My little chirping sparrow!

And when the morn wakes up to see
  My apple bright, my soul's delight!
The partridge shall come calling thee,
  My jar of milk-and-honey!
Yes, thou shalt know what mystery lies
In the amethyst deep of the curtained skies,
If thou wilt fold thy onyx eyes,
  You wakeful one, you naughty son,
    You cooing little turtle!

CHRISTMAS TREASURES

I COUNT my treasures o'er with care,—
  The little toy my darling knew,
  A little sock of faded hue,
A little lock of golden hair.

Long years ago this holy time,
  My little one — my all to me —
  Sat robed in white upon my knee,
And heard the merry Christmas chime.

" Tell me, my little golden-head,
  If Santa Claus should come to-night,
  What shall he bring my baby bright,—
What treasure for my boy?" I said.

And then he named this little toy,
    While in his round and mournful eyes
    There came a look of sweet surprise,
That spake his quiet, trustful joy.

And as he lisped his evening prayer
    He asked the boon with childish grace;
    Then, toddling to the chimney-place,
He hung this little stocking there.

That night, while lengthening shadows crept,
    I saw the white-winged angels come
    With singing to our lowly home
And kiss my darling as he slept.

They must have heard his little prayer,
    For in the morn, with rapturous face,
    He toddled to the chimney-place,
And found this little treasure there.

They came again one Christmas-tide,—
    That angel host, so fair and white;
    And, singing all that glorious night,
They lured my darling from my side.

A little sock, a little toy,
  A little lock of golden hair,
  The Christmas music on the air,
A watching for my baby boy!

But if again that angel train
  And golden-head come back for me,
  To bear me to Eternity,
My watching will not be in vain.

OH, LITTLE CHILD

Hush, little one, and fold your hands—
   The sun hath set, the moon is high;
The sea is singing to the sands,
      And wakeful posies are beguiled
   By many a fairy lullaby—
      Hush, little child—my little child!

Dream, little one, and in your dreams
   Float upward from this lowly place—
Float out on mellow, misty streams
      To lands where bideth Mary mild,
   And let her kiss thy little face,
      You little child—my little child!

Sleep, little one, and take thy rest—
  With angels bending over thee,
Sleep sweetly on that Father's breast
    Whom our dear Christ hath reconciled—
  But stay not there—come back to me,
  Oh, little child—*my* little child!

GANDERFEATHER'S GIFT

I WAS just a little thing
   When a fairy came and kissed me;
Floating in upon the light
Of a haunted summer night,
Lo, the fairies came to sing
Pretty slumber songs and bring
   Certain boons that else had missed me
From a dream I turned to see
What those strangers brought for me,
   When that fairy up and kissed me—
   Here, upon this cheek, he kissed me!

Simmerdew was there, but she
   Did not like me altogether;
Daisybright and Turtledove,
Pilfercurds and Honeylove,
Thistleblow and Amberglee
On that gleaming, ghostly sea

Floated from the misty heather,
And around my trundle-bed
Frisked, and looked, and whispering said —
　Solemnlike and all together:
" *You* shall kiss him, Ganderfeather!"

Ganderfeather kissed me then —
　Ganderfeather, quaint and merry!
No attenuate sprite was he,
— But as buxom as could be; —
Kissed me twice, and once again,
And the others shouted when
　On my cheek uprose a berry
Somewhat like a mole, mayhap,
But the kiss-mark of that chap
　Ganderfeather, passing merry —
　Humorsome, but kindly, very!

I was just a tiny thing
　When the prankish Ganderfeather
Brought this curious gift to me
With his fairy kisses three;
Yet with honest pride I sing

That same gift he chose to bring
  Out of yonder haunted heather.
Other charms and friendships fly—
Constant friends this mole and I,
  Who have been so long together.
Thank you, little Ganderfeather!

BAMBINO

Bambino in his cradle slept;
  And by his side his grandam grim
Bent down and smiled upon the child,
  And sung this lullaby to him,—
    This "ninna and anninia":

" When thou art older, thou shalt mind
  To traverse countries far and wide,
And thou shalt go where roses blow
  And balmy waters singing glide—
    So ninna and anninia!

" And thou shalt wear, trimmed up in points,
  A famous jacket edged in red,
And, more than that, a peakéd hat,
  All decked in gold, upon thy head—
    Ah! ninna and anninia!

" Then shalt thou carry gun and knife,
   Nor shall the soldiers bully thee;
Perchance, beset by wrong or debt,
   A mighty bandit thou shalt be —
     So ninna and anninia!

" No woman yet of our proud race
   Lived to her fourteenth year unwed;
The brazen churl that eyed a girl
   Bought her the ring or paid his head —
     So ninna and anninia!

" But once came spies (I know the thieves!)
   And brought disaster to our race;
God heard us when our fifteen men
   Were hanged within the market-place—
     But ninna and anninia!

" Good men they were, my babe, and true,—
   Right worthy fellows all, and strong;
Live thou and be for them and me
   Avenger of that deadly wrong—
     So ninna and anninia!"

LITTLE HOMER'S SLATE

AFTER dear old grandma died,
   Hunting through an oaken chest
In the attic, we espied
   What repaid our childish quest;
'T was a homely little slate,
Seemingly of ancient date.

On its quaint and battered face
   Was the picture of a cart,
Drawn with all that awkward grace
   Which betokens childish art;
But what meant this legend, pray:
" Homer drew this yesterday"?

Mother recollected then
  What the years were fain to hide —
She was but a baby when
  Little Homer lived and died;
Forty years, so mother said,
Little Homer had been dead.

This one secret through those years
  Grandma kept from all apart,
Hallowed by her lonely tears
  And the breaking of her heart;
While each year that sped away
Seemed to her but yesterday.

So the homely little slate
  Grandma's baby's fingers pressed,
To a memory consecrate,
  Lieth in the oaken chest,
Where, unwilling we should know,
Grandma put it, years ago.